How To Use This Study Guide

This five-lesson study guide corresponds to *"Decoding the Torah — Rick Renner With Guest Rabbi Kirt Schneider"* (Renner TV). Each lesson in this study guide covers a topic that is addressed during the program series, with questions and references supplied to draw you deeper into your own private study of the Scriptures on this subject.

To derive the most benefit from this study guide, consider the following:

First, watch or listen to the program prior to working through the corresponding lesson in this guide. (Programs can also be viewed at **renner.org** by clicking on the Media/Archives links or on our Renner Ministries YouTube channel.)

Second, take the time to look up the scriptures included in each lesson. Prayerfully consider their application to your own life.

Third, use a journal or notebook to make note of your answers to each lesson's Study Questions and Practical Application challenges.

Fourth, invest specific time in prayer and in the Word of God to consult with the Holy Spirit. Write down the scriptures or insights He reveals to you.

Finally, take action! Whatever the Lord tells you to do according to His Word, do it.

For added insights on this subject, it is recommended that you obtain Rabbi Kirt Schneider's book *Decoding the Torah — Applying Ancient Wisdom in a Modern World* by placing your order at **renner.org** or by calling 1-800-742-5593.

TOPIC

Can Rabbinic Law Apply Today?

SCRIPTURES

1. **Matthew 5:17** (*NASB1995*) — Do not think that I came to abolish the Law or the Prophets; I did not come to abolish but to fulfill.
2. **2 Timothy 3:16** (*NASB1995*) — All Scripture is inspired by God and profitable for teaching, for reproof, for correction, for training in righteousness.
3. **Exodus 25:8** (*NASB1995*) — Let them construct a sanctuary for Me, that I may dwell among them.
4. **1 Peter 2:5** — Ye also, as lively stones, are built up a spiritual house, an holy priesthood, to offer up spiritual sacrifices, acceptable to God by Jesus Christ.
5. **John 14:23** (*NASB1995*) — …"If anyone loves Me, he will keep My word; and My Father will love him, and We will come to him and make Our abode with him."
6. **James 4:8** (*NASB1995*) — Draw near to God and He will draw near to you….
7. **Leviticus 10:6** (*NASB1995*) — Then Moses said to Aaron and to his sons Eleazar and Ithamar, "Do not uncover your heads nor tear your clothes…."

GREEK/HEBREW WORDS

"Torah" — meaning instruction; refers to the first five books of the Old Testament, also known as the Pentateuch

SYNOPSIS

The five lessons in this study titled, *Decoding the Torah — Rick Renner With Guest Rabbi Kirt Schneider* will focus on the following topics:

- Can Rabbinic Law Apply Today?
- How Does Jesus Fulfill the Law?

A Note From Rick Renner

I am on a personal quest to see a "revival of the Bible" so people can establish their lives on a firm foundation that will stand strong and endure the test as end-time storm winds begin to intensify.

In order to experience a revival of the Bible in your personal life, it is important to take time each day to read, receive, and apply its truths to your life. James tells us that if we will continue in the perfect law of liberty — refusing to be forgetful hearers, but determined to be doers — we will be blessed in our ways. As you watch or listen to the programs in this series and work through this corresponding study guide, I trust you will search the Scriptures and allow the Holy Spirit to help you hear something new from God's Word that applies specifically to your life. I encourage you to be a doer of the Word He reveals to you. Whatever the cost, I assure you — it will be worth it.

> Thy words were found, and I did eat them;
> and thy word was unto me the joy and rejoicing of mine heart:
> for I am called by thy name, O Lord God of hosts.
> — Jeremiah 15:16

Your brother and friend in Jesus Christ,

Rick Renner

Decoding the Torah

Copyright © 2025 by Teaching You Can Trust, LLC
1814 W. Tacoma St.
Broken Arrow, OK 74012-1406

Published by Rick Renner Ministries
www.renner.org

ISBN 13: 978-1-6675-1379-9

ISBN 13 eBook: 978-1-6675-1380-5

- What Type of Prayer Pleases God?
- Have We Violated God's Creation?
- Are You Following the Crowd?

Just as Rick has poured himself into studying the Greek New Testament to excavate the hidden gems of truth, Rabbi Kirt Schneider has invested his life in studying the Old Testament Hebrew Scriptures to unpack the deep truths they contain. God has given us His *whole* Word to help us understand who He is — His multifaceted wisdom, His nature, His mercy, and His justice. In this lesson, we will see the often-overlooked value of the Old Testament and how rabbinical Law helps us apply the New Testament teachings of Christ and the apostles to our lives.

The emphasis of this lesson:

The Torah is the divine instruction found in the first five books of the Old Testament. It is still relevant and valuable in helping us understand the nature of God and how to live the Christian life laid out in the New Testament. Everyone who studies the Torah will gain deep revelation of how to walk with God.

What Is the 'Torah'?

To begin, we need to know what the Torah is. The Torah, also known as the Pentateuch, is the first five books of our Bible: Genesis, Exodus, Leviticus, Numbers, and Deuteronomy. Unfortunately, when many people hear the word "Torah," they think it just refers to the Law. But the word "Torah" actually means *instruction*, which means way more than just the Law.

Therefore, part of the Torah involves what God said and what took place *before* the Law was given. When we go to the book of Genesis, we find biblical accounts of people and events that took place *before* the Law. For example, Abraham and Sarah's story is in Genesis, so part of the Torah is the calling of Abraham. The same can be said of Noah and the Flood, the tower of Babel, and the record of Jacob and his 12 sons. All of these took place before the Law, and all are a part of the Torah.

A Misunderstanding Made by Many Believers

There is value in "decoding the Torah" in that it enables us to discover what many believers in the Church have missed. As a result of wrong teaching, including antisemitic theology, many Christians have the mindset, "We are not under the Law anymore because Jesus redeemed us from the curse of the Law." While that is 100 percent true, there is a problem that comes with this thinking.

Yes, Jesus redeemed us from the curse of the Law, but that doesn't mean the Law is no longer relevant or valuable. It is still relevant and valuable. Jesus Himself said, "Do not think that I came to abolish the Law or the Prophets; I did not come to abolish but to fulfill" (Matthew 5:17 *NASB1995*). He went on to say, "Whoever therefore breaks one of the least of these commandments, and teaches men so, shall be called least in the kingdom of heaven; but whoever does and teaches them, he shall be called great in the kingdom of heaven" (Matthew 5:19 *NKJV*).

Notice Jesus is speaking about the kingdom of Heaven, which is the age that we're in and the age to come. In this verse, He says "whoever breaks God's commandments." When Jesus says "whoever," He isn't referring to just the Israelites who are legally under the Law but to *anyone* that rejects the self-revelation of Jesus as God. Jesus taught that those who reject the Law and teach others to do so will be called *least* in the kingdom of Heaven. On the other hand, He said those that keep the commandments and teach others to do so will be called *great* in the kingdom of Heaven.

All Scripture Is God-Inspired… Including the Old Testament

Again, the kingdom of Heaven is the age we're in now and it's the age that is to come. The revelation of Jesus and the heart of the Father are in the Torah. Yes, as Christians, we're not under the Law, but let's not abandon the wisdom of the Law. Remember what the apostle Paul wrote under the inspiration of the Holy Spirit:

> **All Scripture is inspired by God and profitable for teaching, for reproof, for correction, for training in righteousness.**
> — 2 Timothy 3:16 (*NASB1995*)

What is interesting is that one verse earlier, in Second Timothy 3:15, Paul told Timothy, "…From a child thou hast known the holy scriptures…." When we read this in the original Greek text, the word "scriptures" is not the word for a scripture. Rather, it is the term that describes *every little jot and every little tittle in the text.*

The use of this word is the equivalent of Paul saying, "Timothy, you were taught from childhood not just to love the Scriptures but to love and have reverence for every letter — every dotted 'i' and every crossed 't'." And the Scriptures Paul is referring to here is *the Old Testament*. The New Testament had not been written and compiled yet.

Friend, the Old Testament was not just written for the people of Israel — it was written also for us. Paul confirms this in his first letter to the Corinthian believers where he said, "Now these things happened to them as an example, and they were written for our instruction, upon whom the ends of the ages have come" (1 Corinthians 10:11 *NASB1995*). "These things" that Paul is talking about are the written accounts of the Old Testament. They were written for our instruction, including those of us who are living at the end of the age.

So everyone who studies the Torah is going to gain deep revelation on how to walk with God. Yes, the New Testament provides powerful, rich teaching on the grace, love, and mercy of God, and it is beautiful! At the same time, there is a treasure trove of divine instruction in the Old Testament that many of God's people have not been exposed to.

When we study the Torah and the rest of the Old Testament, it teaches us how to walk out the great principles of the New Testament. It shows us what it looks like to live in relationship with God and reveals the little details of how to love Him and love others and live a holy life. It teaches us things about how to dress, eat, and reconcile conflicts with others in a way that pleases the Father.

Building a 'Sanctuary' for God

A careful study of the Torah reveals that it contains 613 laws. In his book *Decoding the Torah*, Rabbi Schneider focuses on 100 of these laws as a way of taking a first step toward a greater understanding of the timeless wisdom of God in these Old Testament gems and how they have great application to our lives as New Testament disciples of Jesus.

One law that Rabbi Schneider examines is the law regarding *building a sanctuary for God*. He points to Exodus 25:8 (*NASB1995*), which says, "Let them construct a sanctuary for Me, that I may dwell among them."

What really jumps off the page of the Hebrew Scriptures in this verse is the word "sanctuary." The Lord said, "Construct a sanctuary for Me," and the Hebrew word for "sanctuary" is *miqdas*. It is the word for *a sacred place, a sanctuary*, or *a holy place*. It's a dwelling place of God — referring to *the tabernacle or the temple*.

The Lord instructed Moses to build Him a "sanctuary" so that He might dwell among His people. So in the Hebrew Scriptures, the sanctuary is where God met His people, and every part of the sanctuary was designed by God Himself. In other words, the Israelites didn't just get together and say, "Hey, let's build a house for God," and then erect whatever they thought would be cool.

On the contrary, God said, "I want a curtain fence around everything to be this long, this wide, and this high. I want a bronze altar in front to be made in such-and-such a way along with a bronze basin. Then I want you to build a tent in which I will meet you. It is to have two sections — the front section will be called the Holy Place, and the innermost part is to be the Most Holy Place. And these are the pieces of furniture I want you to build and place within these areas...."

God was the Architect of every aspect of the tabernacle, and every single part of it has significance that is relevant to our life today. Although we no longer build physical tabernacles or temples for God to dwell in, there are prophetic applications for us to learn from in these Old Testament Scriptures.

God's House Is Made of 'Living Stones'

The Old Testament command to build the Lord a sanctuary brings to mind what the apostle Peter wrote in First Peter 2:5, where he declared:

> **Ye also, as lively stones, are built up a spiritual house, an holy priesthood, to offer up spiritual sacrifices, acceptable to God by Jesus Christ.**

Most scholars believe that by the time that Peter wrote this epistle, the Temple in Jerusalem had already been destroyed by the Romans. By writing this, Peter was basically saying, "Brothers and sisters, the old temple is gone, but God still wants to dwell among His people. He is now building a new house, and that house is made up of living stones!" Those living stones are believers from every land and language — everyone that calls on the name of the Lord to be saved. We are part of the building materials that God is using to construct a new temple.

The New Testament gives three metaphors for the Church. One is the *Body of Christ*, which is described in places like Romans 12:5 and First Corinthians 12:27. The second comparison is *a vineyard*, which is probably best explained by Jesus in John 15:1-8. The third and most recurring metaphor for the Church in the entire New Testament is *a temple*. Repeatedly, Scripture says that God is building a temple, and as His temple, we are to be a "habitation for God through the Spirit" (*see* Ephesians 2:22). Hence, God is still wanting to build a habitation among His people.

This symbol of a temple is directly connected with writings in the Torah. When you read through the first five books of the Old Testament — especially Exodus and Leviticus — you see the rich imagery of all the functions of the priesthood and the sacrifices they made in the Temple. God gives specific guidelines and instructions in the Torah.

The Tabernacle, Temple, and Priesthood

When the children of Israel were in the wilderness, God gave them instructions to build the "tabernacle," which in Hebrew is the word *miskan*. After they entered and settled into the Promised Land, the land that became known as Israel, they later converted the temporary tabernacle into the permanent structure called the Temple, which was built by King Solomon. The Temple was patterned after the tabernacle, and the Old Testament tabernacle was patterned after the tabernacle in Heaven (*see* Hebrews 8:1-5).

The point is that these guidelines for the tabernacle, temple worship, and priesthood were very specific. Now, as New Testament believers, we are the temple of the Holy Spirit (*see* 1 Corinthians 3:16), and we are God's holy priests on earth (*see* 1 Peter 2:9). That said, we need to take our calling and service to the Lord seriously.

The truth is there is much we can learn from the laws in the Torah that govern the priesthood and the worship that took place in the tabernacle and Temple. The priests who served were separated and set apart as holy for God's holy purposes. They were guided by very specific instructions regarding how they lived, what they wore, and the way they carried themselves.

There's Much We Can Learn From the Torah

As God's people, we can learn a great deal from what is written in the Torah about how to live a holy life. Unfortunately, we live in a culture that some might call "greasy grace" and "sloppy agape." The standards of holiness among believers have become so watered down and relaxed that in some cases those who claim to be Christians look just like the non-Christians of the world. Many simply don't know how to live holy, separated lives unto God.

Knowing that the Lord told Israel to build Him a tabernacle so that He could dwell among them, we need to stop and ask ourselves, "Is there something that we as God's priests need to do today to make Him feel more welcome in His temple, which is us?" Jesus Himself answers this in large part by telling us plainly:

> ...If anyone loves Me, *he will keep My word*; and My Father will love him, and We will come to him and make Our home with him.
> — John 14:23 (*NKJV*)

What are we to do to make the Lord feel welcome and at home in us, His temple? Jesus said **we are to keep His Word.**

Sadly, there are many Christians who hold to the belief that we don't have to do anything at all to experience God's presence. Although our salvation and everything else we receive from God is a free gift of grace, there are New Testament standards that God calls us to uphold in order to walk in the fullness of His presence and power.

For example, James 4:8 (*NKJV*) says, "Draw near to God and He will draw near to you...." Without question, the Lord wants His presence to rest upon us, but the fullness of who He is can only be experienced when we're walking in alignment with Him. The laws of the Torah give us insight on how to live in aligned relationship with Him. True, we are not legally bound to the Law, but there are powerful truths that we can take and prophetically apply in our own lives today.

The Priests Were To Take Care of Their Appearance

Another law from the Torah that Rabbi Schneider parallels with our Christian life is God's command to the priests to take care of their appearance. This is found in Leviticus 10:6 (*NASB1995*), which says:

> **Then Moses said to Aaron and to his sons Eleazar and Ithamar, "Do not uncover your heads nor tear your clothes...."**

The biblical context of this verse is very important. Moses gave this instruction immediately after God judged Nadab and Abihu for offering up strange incense and fire to Him (*see* Leviticus 10:1-5). The reason the Lord instructed Moses to tell the priests not to uncover their heads or tear their clothes was to show that they were in unity with what God did.

If the priests had ripped out their hair and ripped their clothes over what God did, they would have given the appearance that they were in mourning and disagreed with what He did, and God did not want his priests to mourn the deaths of the disobedient and blasphemous. God needed His priests to stand in solidarity with His judgment. By *not* tearing their clothes and questioning God's actions, the priests helped God's people put their trust in God's righteous judgment.

Keep in mind Judaism is a religion of great study, and Jewish people have gone over these laws for thousands of years trying to extract every minute detail of application. From this law dealing with not tearing their clothes, the rabbis concluded that one of the main principles here is for priests to take care of their appearance. Think about it. If a priest walked around with his hair and clothes disheveled, wreaking of body odor because he hadn't bathed, and presenting himself in an unhealthy way, it would cause God's people to doubt His character.

What Are You Communicating Through Your Appearance?

Likewise, for us today who are God's *royal priesthood*, we need to remember that we are God's visible representatives in the earth. Just like the priests in Moses and Aaron's day were God's visible representatives, we are to represent God in such a way that people are inspired to put their faith in Him and give Him their allegiance.

As God's people, we need to think about how we're dressing and the way we're taking care of ourselves. Is it inspiring faith in God's people? Or are we walking around looking unkept, doubtful, defeated, and depleted of faith? Grooming and personal hygiene are still important and so is maintaining a heart of faith and hope. One of the last things you would want is for someone to look at you and think, *Gee, if that person knows God, why doesn't he (or she) take care of himself? Why does he not take regular showers, wash his hair, and wear clean clothes? If that's what it means to be a Christian, count me out.*

Indeed, it is disturbing how even some preachers dress today. Instead of having an honorable appearance as they stand in the pulpit, many are dressed in worn and torn clothes. They look like they are ready for the beach — not to stand and preach. What's interesting is the word "preach" in Greek describes *the official spokesman of a king*. In New Testament times, to be the king's official spokesman required several things. You had to be cultured, know how to speak to people, and know how *not* to speak to people. You also had to be careful to accurately represent what the king told you to say and dress in a fashion that represented his splendor.

In our next lesson, we explore more about our role as God's representatives and how Jesus was God's ultimate ambassador who came to fulfill the Law, not do away with it.

STUDY QUESTIONS

Study to shew thyself approved unto God, a workman that needeth not to be ashamed, rightly dividing the word of truth.
— 2 Timothy 2:15

1. The most recurring symbol for the Church in the entire New Testament is *a temple*. Repeatedly, Scripture says that God is building a temple, and *we* are His temple. Take a moment to read these amazing verses declaring how we are a "habitation for God's Spirit" (*see* Ephesians 2:22).
    * First Corinthians 3:16
    * First Corinthians 6:19
    * Second Corinthians 6:16
    * Ephesians 2:19-22

2. To make the Lord feel welcome and at home in us, His temple, Jesus said we are to *keep His Word* (*see* John 14:23). In our own ability, we can't obey and keep God's Word. But if we will *humble* ourselves and ask Him for help daily, He will give us His *grace* to live a righteous life! Take time to meditate on these promises and begin to humbly pray for God's grace to crucify your flesh and live holy!
    But He gives us more and more grace (power of the Holy Spirit, to meet this evil tendency and all others fully). That is why He says, God sets Himself against the proud and haughty, but gives

grace [continually] to the lowly (those who are humble enough to receive it).

— James 4:6 (*AMPC*)

…Clothe (apron) yourselves, all of you, with humility [as the garb of a servant, so that its covering cannot possibly be stripped from you, with freedom from pride and arrogance] toward one another. For God sets Himself against the proud (the insolent, the overbearing, the disdainful, the presumptuous, the boastful) — [and He opposes, frustrates, and defeats them], but gives grace (favor, blessing) to the humble.

— 1 Peter 5:5 (*AMPC*)

For if you live according to [the dictates of] the flesh, you will surely die. But if *through the power of the [Holy] Spirit* you are [habitually] putting to death (making extinct, deadening) the [evil] deeds prompted by the body, you shall [really and genuinely] live forever.

— Romans 8:13 (*AMPC*)

I have strength for all things in Christ Who empowers me [I am ready for anything and equal to anything through Him Who infuses inner strength into me; I am self-sufficient in Christ's sufficiency].

— Philippians 4:13 (*AMPC*)

PRACTICAL APPLICATION

But be ye doers of the word, and not hearers only, deceiving your own selves.
— James 1:22

1. What was your perception of the "Torah" prior to this lesson? Had you ever heard of it? How is the Holy Spirit re-shaping your understanding of this vital part of God's Word?

2. In what ways has the Old Testament, including the first five books (Torah), impacted your life? What Old Testament passages and principles stand out as having brought more clarity and meaning to the teachings of the New Testament? How is it showing you how to live in relationship with God?

3. Have you heard it taught that we are "not under the Law anymore because Jesus redeemed us from the curse of the Law"? While this is true, what problems can you now see developing from this kind of thinking?

TOPIC

How Does Jesus Fulfill the Law?

SCRIPTURES

1. **Matthew 1:1** (*NIV*) — This is the genealogy of Jesus the Messiah the son of David, the son of Abraham.

2. **John 1:16-17** — And of his fulness have all we received, and grace for grace. For the law was given by Moses, but grace and truth came by Jesus Christ.

3. **John 1:16-17** (*NKJV*) — And of His fullness we have all received, and grace for grace. For the law was given through Moses, *but* grace and truth came through Jesus Christ.

4. **John 1:16-17** (*NASB1995*) — For of His fullness we have all received, and grace upon grace. For the Law was given through Moses; grace and truth were realized through Jesus Christ.

5. **Leviticus 10:6** (*NASB1995*) — Then Moses said to Aaron and to his sons Eleazar and Ithamar, "Do not uncover your heads nor tear your clothes...."

6. **Exodus 20:26** (*NASB1995*) — And you shall not go up by steps to My altar, so that your nakedness will not be exposed on it.

7. **Exodus 30:9** (*NASB1995*) — You shall not offer any strange incense on this altar, or burnt offering or meal offering; and you shall not pour out a drink offering on it.

GREEK/HEBREW WORDS

1. "Torah" — meaning instruction; refers to the first five books of the Old Testament, also known as the Pentateuch

2. "preacher" — κῆρυξ (*kerux*): a herald or spokesman of the king

SYNOPSIS

As a believer, it is very important to know Jesus' connection with the Law, which God gave through Moses. Christ Himself said, "Don't misunderstand why I have come. I did not come to abolish the law of Moses or the writings of the prophets. No, I came to accomplish their purpose" (Matthew 5:17 *NLT*). So Jesus didn't throw the Torah and the Old Testament in the trash when He came. Rather, His life, death, and resurrection are the fulfillment of everything that was written.

Indeed, they are so vitally important that He went on to say in the very next verse, "I tell you the truth, until heaven and earth disappear, not even the smallest detail of God's law will disappear until its purpose is achieved" (Matthew 5:18 *NLT*). Jesus Christ is the embodiment and fulfillment of the Old Testament Scriptures! And while we no longer follow its sacrificial system, the Scriptures do provide unmatched insights into who God is and how we are to relate to Him and others.

The emphasis of this lesson:

Jesus is the continuation and embodiment of the Torah. He didn't come to abolish the Law but to fulfill it. The Law of God is the foundation of God's grace upon which the fullness of His grace in Christ rests. As we value and study the Old Testament Scriptures, a healthy, holy fear of the Lord will be restored in our lives.

The Torah Provides Instruction We Can't Get Elsewhere

There is something God wants to restore in the lives of His people today. As a result of wrong teaching and the absence of sound, biblical doctrine, many believers are disconnected from the Hebrew roots of their faith, including the Law of God or the Torah. God wants that to change!

Keep in mind, as we learned in Lesson 1, the word "Torah" means *instruction*, and it refers to the first five books of the Old Testament, also known as the Pentateuch. So when you read and study the Torah, you are going to receive divine *instruction*. In fact, feeding your spirit the Torah will put something in you that you can't get by just reading the New Testament. It is self-revealing.

The Torah is so valuable that the New Testament begins by quoting it. In Matthew 1:1 (*NIV*), the Scripture says, "This is the genealogy of Jesus the Messiah the son of David, the son of Abraham." Matthew goes on for 17 verses, reciting the family lineage from Abraham, the father of faith, all the way to Jesus, the Messiah.

Thus Jesus is the continuation, the embodiment, and the fulfillment of the Torah. It was so vital in His estimation that He said whoever does what the commandments and the prophets say and teaches them to others, "…He shall be called *great* in the kingdom of heaven" (Matthew 5:19 *NKJV*).

Antisemitism Has Influenced Christianity for Hundreds of Years

Tragically, antisemitism crept into the Church very early. For example, in the Fourth Century, Constantine, who was the ruler of the Roman Empire, became an antisemite. Although he declared Christianity to be the religion of the Roman Empire, which stopped the persecution of Christians, his antisemitic bent moved him to purposely try to separate Christianity from its Jewish roots.

For instance, he tried to outlaw the celebration of certain Jewish holy days. Decisions like this and others set the Church on a path that led them away from the Torah, and as a result — for hundreds and hundreds of years — well-meaning, sincere believers that were hungry for God didn't have an opportunity nor were they encouraged to learn the Torah and its applicability for their life today.

This antisemitic influence runs so deep that it influenced the translators of the *King James Version* of the Bible. This beautiful, classic translation of Scripture — possibly the most influential version of the Bible worldwide that's ever been written — was impacted by an underlying prejudice against the people of Israel.

Is the Law 'Anti-Grace'?

A primary example of this antisemitic influence on the translators of the *King James Version* is seen clearly in how John 1:16 and 17 were translated. Here is how it reads in the *King James Version*:

And of his fulness have all we received, and grace for grace. For the law was given by Moses, *but* grace and truth came by Jesus Christ.

Notice it says, "And of his fullness have we all received," which means out of the fullness or abundance of what Jesus Christ has, all of us have received. Specifically, we have received "grace for grace."

John went on to say, "For the law was given by Moses, *but* grace and truth came by Jesus Christ" (John 1:17). Please note the word "but." Its use here sets up a contrast between what Moses gave and what Jesus gave to us. It sounds like the Law that came through Moses is opposite or in contrast to the grace that came to us through Jesus. That is what is implied by the inclusion of the word "but" in the *King James Version*.

Consider this example. You and your spouse go to dinner together and enjoy some delicious food. The downside is that it took an hour for the food to get to your table after you ordered it. Later that evening, as the manager of the restaurant is making his rounds, he comes over to your table and asks, "How was the meal?" In response, you say, "Well, the food was delicious, *but* the service was poor." The word "but" sets up a contrast between the food that was so good and the service, which was poor.

That is what is happening when we read the *King James Version* of John 1:17:

For the law was given by Moses, *but* grace and truth came by Jesus Christ.

The Law that was given to us by Moses appears to be *opposite* or *not as good as* the grace that came by Jesus. But if you look carefully at John 1:17 in the *King James Version* of the Bible, you'll see that the word "but" is in *italics*, and the reason it is in italics is because it was added by the translators. A note, usually in the front or back of the *King James Version* states that words in italics were supplied by the translators to help make the meaning of the passages clearer.

So although the translators were trying to help us understand what Moses and Jesus brought, because they had been unknowingly influenced by wrong theology going all the way back to the antisemitism of Constantine, they thought the Law was anti-grace. When in fact, just the opposite is true.

The Law or Torah
Is 'Foundational Grace'

Looking at these same two verses in other Bible versions helps to clarify what the Holy Spirit is telling us through the apostle John. When we look at John 1:16 and 17 in the *New American Standard Bible 1995*, this passage reads:

> **For of His fullness we have all received, and grace upon grace. For the Law was given through Moses; grace and truth were realized through Jesus Christ.**

First, notice that the Bible says from His — Jesus' — fullness, we have all received, and we have specifically received *grace* upon *grace*. Here we see one grace stacked on top of another grace.

Then as we continue in verse 17, it says, "For the Law was given through Moses; grace and truth were realized through Jesus Christ." This verse identifies the "two graces" described in verse 16. The first grace was *the Law* — it was an elementary grace or preparatory grace. It is the foundation that the fullness of grace was placed upon.

Thus, the law is *not* opposite grace — it is an elementary or foundational grace.

The second grace is the *grace and truth* that came through Jesus. The fullness of God's grace was realized through Jesus, but an elementary grace had already come into the world through the Law. This makes it clear that the Law is not anti-grace. The Law is a preparatory and administrative grace that teaches us how to walk out the earthly nitty-gritty details of our life. Thus the Torah has application for us today.

If you think about the world at the time when the Law came, it was a pagan world without any rules. It was a world of chaos where every man did what he wanted to do and what seemed right in his own eyes. But when God began to speak and provided His Law, or rules, it began to create boundaries that provided safety and loving protection. This is why it is wrong for people to just ignore and discount the Torah and the Old Testament and say it's not important. It is still very important, and there's so much for us to gain from it.

God Commanded His Priests
To Take Care of Their Appearance

In Lesson 1, we learned about what the Torah is and delved into a few commands found in the Torah. There are 613 commands in the Torah, and one of those commands deals with the priests taking care of their appearance. Here again is what the Bible says:

> **Then Moses said to Aaron and to his sons Eleazar and Ithamar, "Do not uncover your heads nor tear your clothes...."**
> **— Leviticus 10:6 (*NASB1995*)**

We saw that this command Moses gave was immediately after God had judged Nadab and Abihu, two of Aaron's priestly sons that had offered up strange incense to God (*see* Leviticus 10:1-5). The reason the Lord instructed Moses to tell the priests not to uncover their heads, which meant to rip out their hair, or tear their clothes was to show that they were in support of God's righteous judgment.

If the priests had ripped out their hair and torn their clothes to mourn what God did, they would have given the appearance that they were questioning God and not in agreement with His actions. By maintaining their composure and their appearance, the priests communicated to God's people that He was right in what He did, and they should trust Him.

As Believers
We Are God's 'Holy Priests'

Flash forward to the New Testament, and we see that as born-again children of God, we are God's *priests*. First Peter 2:9 (*TLB*) says, "...For you have been chosen by God himself — you are priests of the King, you are holy and pure, you are God's very own — all this so that you may show to others how God called you out of the darkness into his wonderful light."

As God's "priests" serving on the earth today, we are to be mindful of our appearance and take good care of how we dress. Although Rick and Rabbi Schneider were in no way trying to be hurtful or offensive to anyone, they expressed deep concern over the way some believers — including people in leadership — are dressing when they go to church. It seems many Christians these days are dressed more for the beach or a picnic than for entering the presence of God.

Think about how you would dress if you were invited to the oval office to meet the president of the United States. Would you wear ripped jeans, sandals, a T-shirt, or shorts? Probably not. The truth is, you would put on your best suit or dress, your best shirt and shoes, and have your hair fixed and looking its best. Why? Because you are coming into the presence of the President.

Should we do anything less when we come into the presence of God, the greatest leader in the universe? The way we dress really shows what and who we respect.

Leadership Has Its Privileges, and It Also Has Responsibilities

How about our church leaders? Is the way they dress important? Absolutely. Take for example those who *preach* the Word. The Greek word for "preacher" in the New Testament is *kerux*, and it describes *a herald or spokesman of the king*. When a person served as the king's spokesman, he was obligated to represent him well. This person had to accurately repeat what the king told him to say, and he could not add his own words or interpretation.

The spokesman of the king (*kerux*) would also not tell jokes and entertain people because he was speaking on behalf of the king. Moreover, this individual had to know how to be cultured and polite when he spoke to people because if he was rude, it would be a poor reflection on the king. Furthermore, the king's spokesman had to know how to bring correction; he needed to be able to give it sternly but also compassionately. And he needed to dress honorably in a way that reflected the royalty he was representing. If he stood in front of the citizens of the kingdom or foreign dignitaries dressed in shoddy clothes, that would be an insult and likely be the last time he ever spoke on the king's behalf.

All who are "preachers" (*kerux*) are spokesmen of King Jesus, and these guidelines apply to them. Sadly, many have lost respect for who God is, who they are in Him, and what our purpose is on the earth — to represent Him with excellence. When we speak for God, we should reflect who we are representing.

Think about Moses and Joshua who were both called to represent God before the nation of Israel. When they came into God's presence, the Lord told them to take off their shoes, for they were standing on holy ground (*see* Exodus 3:5; Joshua 5:15). Like them, we need to understand who God is, have a holy reverence and appreciation for Him, and understand our calling as His priests on earth. This is a heart issue — not a legalistic issue.

The Church Needs a Fresh Infusion of the Fear of the Lord

One of the blessings that comes from studying the Law is that it restores to us a holy reverence for the Lord. The Church today, by and large, really needs a super-sized dose of the holy fear of the Lord. Although some in the Church have said, "We've been delivered from the fear of the Lord," and "We don't fear Him anymore because we have Jesus now," that is not true. The Bible clearly states:

> …**Work out your own salvation with *fear and trembling*.**
> — **Philippians 2:12**

For the record, that is what Paul wrote in the New Testament. He also said, "It is because of this solemn *fear of the Lord*, which is ever present in our minds, that we work so hard to win others…" (2 Corinthians 5:11 *TLB*), and that as we work for and serve others, we are to "…serve them sincerely because of [our] *reverent fear of the Lord*" (Colossians 3:22 *NLT*). Indeed, the Bible says:

> **The reverent and worshipful fear of the Lord is the beginning (the chief and choice part) of Wisdom, and the knowledge of the Holy One is insight and understanding.**
> — **Proverbs 9:10 (*AMPC*)**

Friend, the holy fear of the Lord is clean and empowering (*see* Psalm 19:9). When Isaiah prophesied about Jesus, He said that upon Him would rest "…the spirit of knowledge and *the fear of the Lord*. And He will delight *in the fear of the Lord*, and He will not judge by what His eyes see, nor make a decision by what His ears hear" (Isaiah 11:2-3 *NASB1995*).

Jesus Himself said:

> **Do not fear those who kill the body but are unable to kill the soul; but rather *fear Him* who is able to destroy both soul and body in hell.**
> — **Matthew 10:28 (*NASB1995*)**

To be clear, Jesus is not saying we are to walk around on eggshells, afraid of God all the time. What He and the other Bible writers are advocating is that each of us cultivate a holy reverential fear and awe of who God is. That is what needs to be restored to the Church today, and one of the ways this holy fear of the Lord is restored is through studying the Torah and the Old Testament Scriptures.

Modesty Among the Priests Was Mandatory

It is interesting to note that one of the commandments in the Torah dealt specifically with the issue of priests being modest as they served before the Lord. Exodus 20:26 (*NASB1995*) says, "And you shall not go up by steps to My altar, so that your nakedness will not be exposed on it."

To understand this commandment, you need to know that in the ancient world, steps did not have risers. In other words, there were open spaces between each step. So if you were standing on the opposite side of where the priest was walking up the steps to the altar, you'd be able to see underneath his garments, and his nakedness would be exposed.

Essentially, God said, "I don't want the priests' nakedness exposed. It's not proper in my presence." Instead of building steps to the altar, the Israelites were to build a ramp so that no one would be able to see underneath the priests' garments. It's really all about modesty.

The Principle of Modesty Applies to Us Today

When we get dressed to go to a church service, we really need to stop and ask ourselves, *Who am I getting dressed for? Am I dressing to honor and please God? Or am I putting on clothes to draw attention to me and my flesh?* If we are going to church dressed to draw people's attention to us, that is insulting to the Lord.

First Corinthians 1:29 says, "That no flesh should glory in his presence." Sadly, many are coming to worship God — even those on our worship teams who are on the platform and in front of everyone — and they are dressed inappropriately and provocatively. Under the inspiration of the Holy Spirit, Paul wrote:

> **And I want women to be modest in their appearance. They should wear decent and appropriate clothing and not draw**

attention to themselves by the way they fix their hair or by wearing gold or pearls or expensive clothes.

— 1 Timothy 2:9 (*NLT*)

As men and women, we need to love and honor the Lord in the way we dress. Out of reverence for Him, and concern for our fellow brothers and sisters in Christ, we should not be wearing skintight pants, see-through shirts, or any type of sensuous clothing that would cause others to be visually stimulated. We are to dress in such a way that brings God glory and puts the focus on Him.

Yes, as men and as women, each of us are responsible for guarding our eyes and not giving place to a spirit of lust. At the same time, out of sincere love for God and one another, we should never do anything that would cause another brother of sister to fall into sin (*see* Romans 14:21; 15:1). Paul said, "So if what I eat causes another believer to sin, I will never eat meat again as long as I live — for I don't want to cause another believer to stumble" (1 Corinthians 8:13 *NLT*).

So let's be mindful that we represent the Lord and that how we dress does affect other people. If we will pray and ask God for help, He will give us the grace to develop a healthy, reverential fear of Him and genuine love for others. He will show us how to dress attractively, yet modestly, and bring Him glory in all we do.

In our next lesson, we will look at what it means to offer "strange incense and fire" to God.

STUDY QUESTIONS

Study to shew thyself approved unto God, a workman that needeth not to be ashamed, rightly dividing the word of truth.
— 2 Timothy 2:15

1. In addition to being called a "royal priesthood" (1 Peter 2:9), what does the apostle Paul say we are in Second Corinthians 5:20, and what are we called to do? (*See* vv. 18-19.) How are you doing with this calling? What practical steps can you take to come up higher in this area?

2. After reading the *King James Version* of John 1:16-17 and realizing the translators added the word "but," how does this change your

understanding of this passage? What new insights of these verses does the *New American Standard Bible 1995* provide you?

3. What do you know about the **fear of the Lord**? This virtue is instilled and cultivated in us by the Holy Spirit as we continue to abide in relationship with Him and feed on God's Word. What are the benefits and blessings of the fear of the Lord? Take time to ponder these priceless promises:

- Psalm 111:10 and Proverbs 1:7; 9:10

- Psalm 34:7-14; Proverbs 8:13; 16:6

- Psalm 25:12-14; Proverbs 15:33; 19:23

- Psalms 31:19-20; 33:18; 112:1; 128:1

- Proverbs 10:27; 14:26-27; 22:4

PRACTICAL APPLICATION

> But be ye doers of the word, and not hearers only,
> deceiving your own selves.
> —James 1:22

1. Have you ever served under or alongside a Christian leader who took great care in how he dressed, carried himself, and interacted with others? If so, who was it, and how did his example affect you? In contrast, have you ever served under or alongside a Christian leader who was consistently unkempt, had poor hygiene, and didn't carry himself well? How did this person's example affect you and the others with whom he served? What does all this say to you about your appearance?

2. Out of sincere love for God and others we should never do anything that would cause a fellow believer to fall into sin. This principle for living is made clear in Romans 14:12-21; 15:1-2; and First Corinthians 8:9-13. Take some time to carefully read these passages and write what the Holy Spirit speaks to you. If He shows you anything you need to repent of, *repent*. If He shows you any changes you need to make in what you're doing, ask Him for the grace to change it.

TOPIC

What Type of Prayer Pleases God?

SCRIPTURES

1. **Exodus 30:7-8** (*NASB1995*) — Aaron shall burn fragrant incense on it; he shall burn it every morning when he trims the lamps. When Aaron trims the lamps at twilight, he shall burn incense. There shall be perpetual incense before the Lord throughout your generations.

2. **Exodus 30:9** (*NASB1995*) — You shall not offer any strange incense on this altar, or burnt offering or meal offering; and you shall not pour out a drink offering on it.

3. **Psalm 5:3** — My voice shalt thou hear in the morning, O Lord; in the morning will I direct my prayer unto thee, and will look up.

GREEK/HEBREW WORDS

No Greek or Hebrew words were shown on the TV program.

SYNOPSIS

In the tenth chapter of Leviticus, the Bible tells of two of Aaron's sons, Nadab and Abihu, who offered "strange fire" before the Lord, which He had commanded them not to do. And because of their actions, fire went out from the Lord and consumed them (*see* Leviticus 10:1-2). What is this "strange fire"? How is it connected with prayer? And what does this example speak to us today?

The emphasis of this lesson:

Incense in the Old Testament is a symbol of our continual prayer and worship to God. Offering "strange incense" on God's altar would be offering inappropriate prayers to Him. Prayer that pleases God is genuine, sincere, heartfelt prayer directed straight to Him.

Do You Have 'Bells' and 'Pomegranates'?

In our previous two lessons, we have noted that according to the ancient rabbis, the Torah has 613 commandments. That number is significant as it is also connected with the ministry of the high priest. The Bible speaks of how the high priest of Israel wore a flowing garment, and at the bottom of his garment there was a series of alternating bells and pomegranates sewn all around the fringe of his priestly robe. So as the high priest would walk about, the people would hear the bells and they would see the pomegranates.

If you ever visit Israel, one of the first things you may encounter is someone trying to sell you a glass of pomegranate juice, which is delicious and very nourishing. According to Jewish tradition, a pomegranate has *613 seeds* in it — the same number of commandments said to be in the Torah. Whether that is scientifically accurate of every pomegranate is not known. But the fact that pomegranate juice is offered to visitors as they enter the Holy Land is beautifully symbolic.

Even more fascinating is the fact that 3,500 years ago, the Lord commanded the high priests to wear embroidered pomegranates around the fringe of their garments. The alternating pomegranates and tiny bells prophetically picture two things. The bells, which jingled every time the high priest moved, represent our *voice*. Hence, the bell is symbolic of our *verbal witness* in the world. The pomegranates represent the *fruit of the Spirit* in our life.

As believers, we are to have both "bells" and "pomegranates" in our life. In other words, we are to be speaking and telling people about Jesus, and we are to have the fruit of the Spirit available to those around us. This enables people to hear the Gospel and the timeless instruction of God's Word, and at the same time they can taste the fruit of the Spirit and see for themselves that the Lord is good! (*See* Psalm 34:8.)

Incense Was Offered Exclusively to the Lord

Another very unusual command that God gave the people of Israel in the Torah is found in **Exodus 30:9** (*NASB1995*). Here, God said:

> **You shall not offer any strange incense on this altar, or burnt offering or meal offering; and you shall not pour out a drink offering on it.**

There are a few things you need to know about the incense that was offered. First, you need to know that it had to be made of specific ingredients. Exodus 30:34-36 reveals this was a blend of spices, including stacte, onycha, galbanum, and pure frankincense. This very specific mixture was ordained by God and considered holy. It could only be used to offer up to the Lord and was not for anyone's personal use.

This exclusive use of incense to the Lord demonstrated *separation*, *distinction*, and *holiness* unto the Him. That is the way God wants to be treated and regarded. He is separate, distinct, and holy above everything else in our life.

Every morning, the priests were to offer up or burn incense to the Lord in the tabernacle or the temple. The mixture of ingredients was according to the divine prescription God gave, and it was a continual perpetual offering of worship and prayer to the Holy One, Yahweh, the God and Father of the Lord Jesus Christ.

The priests didn't have multiple menorahs burning incense all around the camp of Israel. It was only offered to God in one place and reserved exclusively for Him. If the priests violated this command and offered "strange incense on God's altar," they came under God's judgment, which is what happened to Nadab and Abihu. The Lord struck them down.

What Might Offering 'Strange Incense' Look Like Today?

Incense in the Old Testament is a symbol of our prayer and worship to God. That said, offering "strange incense on the altar" would be offering *strange prayer* to the Lord. This inappropriate prayer would include people praying in such a way that their heart is not really directed to God when they pray. Instead, it is directed elsewhere.

Keep in mind that when the priests burned incense on the altar in the tabernacle or temple, it was burned in an enclosed area where there was no wind. Incense was offered in the Holy Place, which was surrounded by walls and covered by a roof. Therefore, the smoke from the incense went straight up.

In the same way, when we pray and worship God, our prayer is to ascend straight up to Him. Sometimes, however, when people pray, they're not praying in a way that their heart is connected to God. Instead, they're praying to impress the people around them. This seems to happen most often in group settings where individuals will pray in turns, and their prayers are not fully directed upward but are directed in some measure toward each other. Whether knowingly or unknowingly, people begin to spiritually compete to sound more pious or religious than everyone else, and this is offensive to the Lord. This would be one example of "offering strange prayer" to the Lord.

Another example of our prayers not going directly to the Lord as they should is praying in such a way that we are relying on religious traditions and praying prayers that we've heard or memorized that are part of the Christian culture. These are prayers that are not authentic or from the heart. Instead, it's going through the motions and checking a religious box.

Jesus warned about praying useless prayers, telling us, "And when you are praying, do not use meaningless repetition as the Gentiles do, for they suppose that they will be heard for their many words" (Matthew 6:7 NASB1995). He then assured us that God knows what we need before we ask, so we are to just pray to Him straight from the heart.

Fabricating the Anointing

Another example of offering "strange incense" to God is something Rick said he and Denise experienced many years ago. They had been invited to minister at a church that was exploding with growth. When Rick asked the pastor the reason for the church's rapid expansion, the pastor said, "It is because I have a unique sign and wonder. During the service, oil begins to flow from my hands, and it's supernatural. People are coming to see the oil."

That evening, during the service, Rick began to think about what the pastor had said, and he was very disturbed by the whole thing. Then, as he was standing next to the pastor, he looked over at him and saw him reach into his pocket, pull out an oil capsule, and break it on his hands.

"Look!" the pastor exclaimed, "The oil has begun to flow!"

It was fake — the whole thing was a sham! And when Rick saw what the man was doing, the Lord prompted him to speak from the Old Testament about what happens to those who fabricate the anointing. He preached on it all four nights he was at the church.

Make no mistake. Fabricating the anointing is extremely offensive in the eyes of the Lord, and it brings His judgment. This example of offering "strange incense" is serious business and something we are never to do. We really need to guard our hearts and cultivate a healthy habit of praying genuine, heartfelt prayers. They are a sweet fragrance to the Lord.

Our Prayers and Praise Bring God Joy and Pleasure

There is another command in the Torah that talks about burning incense to God, and it's found in Exodus 30. Here the Lord told Moses:

> **Aaron shall burn fragrant incense on it; he shall burn it every morning when he trims the lamps. When Aaron trims the lamps at twilight, he shall burn incense. There shall be perpetual incense before the Lord throughout your generations.**
> **— Exodus 30:7-8 (*NASB1995*)**

When Israel offered the Lord sacrifices according to the direction He had given them, the Lord called it "My offering, My food" and said it was "a sweet aroma" to Him (Numbers 28:2 *NKJV*).

The same thing is true when we offer our prayers of thanksgiving, praise, and worship to the Lord from a pure heart. It is His food! Somehow, our loving words of appreciation are like a sweet, fragrant aroma that blesses Him greatly. Although God is complete in and of Himself and needs nothing, somehow, we add pleasure to His life when we worship Him.

The offering of fragrant incense to the Lord every morning is symbolic of us offering up our hearts to Him in sincere worship and praise. When we cling to Him in love and adoration, expressing our desire to walk with Him at the beginning of our day, somehow it fills His heart with great joy. Jesus said, "...There is joy in the presence of the angels of God over one sinner that repenteth" (Luke 15:10). Similarly, the Father rejoices when we're living our lives surrendered in devotion to Him.

Rick shared how every morning and every evening he and Denise start and end their day with the Lord. The first and last thing they do each day is raise their hands, open their mouths, and bless the Lord from their hearts.

Regardless of How You Feel, Pray and Give God Praise

Do you think the priests woke up every morning feeling happy? No, they didn't. It is safe to say there were many mornings they were feeling groggy, exhausted, discouraged, and maybe even sick. There were probably times they felt disconnected in their heart from God. But regardless of how they felt in their body or in their emotions, every morning they got up and did the same thing. They began their day by worshipping God and offering up sweet-smelling incense.

In Psalm 5:3, David prayed, "My voice shalt thou hear in the morning, O Lord; in the morning will I direct my prayer unto thee, and will look up."

David was a man surrounded with all kinds of problems. He had many enemies and many problems in his family, especially with his kids. Yet he knew if he didn't start the day "looking up," it would just be a matter of minutes until he would be looking down.

Likewise, in the day in which we live, if we don't look up first, our phone is going to *ping*, and we're going to get notifications and messages that are going to upset us. Or our spouse may give us a look that just throws our whole day off. The fact is, it doesn't take much for us to start looking down. That's why we must make the decision to purposely start the day surrendering ourselves to the Lord.

Friend, before you lift your head off the pillow, first look up. Don't look at your phone, your spouse, the news, or anything else until you first look to Jesus. Offer to Him the sweet incense of your prayer of thanksgiving, praise, and worship. It is a sweet-smelling aroma to the Lord that brings joy to His heart and magnetically attracts His unrivaled presence into your life. This is one of the most practical laws in the Torah that you can apply to your life immediately every morning.

Discipline Is What We Need To Succeed

So how can we consistently pray each morning, offering thanksgiving and praise to the Lord? We need *discipline* in our life. Of course, most of us would much rather talk about God's grace and mercy, but discipline is what we need to be effective in all areas of our life. Paul said:

For bodily discipline is only of little profit, but godliness is profitable for all things, since it holds promise for the present life and also for the life to come.

— 1 Timothy 4:8 (*NASB1995*)

The word "godliness" Paul uses here is linked to *spiritual discipline*. It is profitable for all things, not only in this life but also in the life to come. Developing discipline is important to walking in the Spirit.

If you feel like you're an undisciplined person, don't panic, because God can strengthen you and help you become more disciplined. If you ask Him, He will help you cultivate a practice of "burning sweet incense" through offering your heart to Him fresh and new every morning.

In contrast, if you live your life controlled by your emotions, you're going to give up quickly. Let's face it, sometimes you have bad dreams and don't get a good night's sleep, and you wake up feeling weary. Other times you wake up feeling disconnected from God for no known reason, and you just don't feel like praying. If you give in to your feelings, you will seldom pray.

Instead, regardless of whether you're feeling emotionally inspired or not, you are to choose to pray. Get up, get alone with God in a designated place, and begin to seek His face. Sometimes putting on worship music can be very helpful in creating an atmosphere of prayer. Be still and let the Holy Spirit minister to you. Then pick up your Bible and begin reading a psalm or two. The psalms are a wonderful reminder of the blessings and kindness of the Lord, giving us reasons to thank Him and praise Him for His mercy and love toward us.

Put Into Practice the Healthy Habit of Prayer

Developing the discipline of praying every morning and committing your day to God will liberate your life and drastically change your day. It is a decision of the will, not a feeling of emotion. Without discipline, people's lives fall to pieces.

For discipline to remain effective, you can't make exceptions or excuses because once you do, the door is opened to compromise, and pretty soon your established routine will have gone out the window.

Discipline is actually your friend, leading you to the good life you want! It will make you healthier, causing you to eat right. It will make you stronger, causing you to exercise regularly. And the discipline of starting and ending each day by looking to the Lord in prayer will really bring the presence of God into your life.

Friend, be encouraged! Put into practice the healthy habit of offering God the incense of your prayers, however He instructs you and leads you to do it, and stick with it. You will be blessed. You'll be stronger, and you'll keep ascending into the Spirit and find yourself living a more empowered life.

STUDY QUESTIONS

> **Study to shew thyself approved unto God, a workman that needeth not to be ashamed, rightly dividing the word of truth.**
> **— 2 Timothy 2:15**

1. God's Word has much to say about prayer. For us, our prayers are the perpetual incense we offer to Him throughout each day of our lives. Look up these select passages, jotting down what the Holy Spirit reveals to you about prayer. What should your prayers include and not include?

    *   **The Lord's Prayer** – Matthew 6:5-15 and Luke 11:1-4
    *   **How often should you pray** – First Thessalonians 5:17; Luke 18:1; Ephesians 6:18
    *   **Persistence is important** – Luke 11:5-13 and Matthew 7:7-11
    *   **Ask in Jesus' name** – John 14:13-14; 15:16; 16:24-27
    *   **The role of the Holy Spirit** – Romans 8:26-27; Jude 20
    *   **Conditions of effective prayer** – Jeremiah 29:12-13; James 5:16; John 15:7; First John 5:14-15

2. How can we consistently pray each morning, offering thanksgiving and praise to the Lord? By developing *discipline* in our life. Although many people view discipline as a dirty word, it is a major sign of God's love. See for yourself what God says about discipline in Hebrews 12:5-11; Isaiah 38:16; and First Corinthians 9:26-27.

PRACTICAL APPLICATION

> But be ye doers of the word, and not hearers only,
> deceiving your own selves.
> — James 1:22

1. David was surrounded by problems. He had many enemies and many challenges in his family. Yet, he knew if he didn't start the day "looking up," in a short time he would be looking down. What do you "look to" first when you get up in the morning? Is it the *news*? *Social media*? *Emails* or *text messages*? If so, how's that working for you? Why not take the next seven days and purposely choose to **look at God first**? Journal what happens when you put prayer, thanksgiving and praise, and reading His Word at the start of each day. The results will be a pleasant surprise.

2. Be honest. Are you offering "strange incense" to God when you pray? Are there times when you're praying more to impress those around you than to connect with the Father? Are you praying prayers you've memorized from religious tradition rather than praying genuinely from your heart? If so, take time to *repent* and ask God to forgive you and to empower you to begin praying sincerely, thanking Him and praising Him for His lovingkindness, mercy, and faithfulness in your life.

LESSON 4

TOPIC
Have We Violated God's Creation?

SCRIPTURES

1. **Leviticus 19:19** (*ESV*) — You shall keep my statutes. You shall not let your cattle breed with a different kind. You shall not sow your field with two kinds of seed, nor shall you wear a garment of cloth made of two kinds of material.

2. **Exodus 23:32-33** (*NASB1995*) — You shall make no covenant with them or with their gods. They shall not live in your land, because they

will make you sin against Me; for if you serve their gods, it will surely be a snare to you.

GREEK/HEBREW WORDS

No Greek or Hebrew words were shown on the TV program.

SYNOPSIS

What did God mean when He told the Israelites, "Don't let your cattle breed with a different kind or plant your field with two kinds of seed"? And what was His reason for telling them not to wear a garment of cloth made of two kinds of material? Why would the Lord give His people such instructions, and what is the significance of these commands to us today?

The emphasis of this lesson:

Leviticus 19:19 is God's command not to tamper with His creation. He's the Architect of the created world, and He wants us to respect the boundaries He has established. But through things like transhumanism, DNA tampering, and the development of AI, mankind has defied God's laws and bought into the same lie the serpent sold to Eve in Eden.

The 'Forbidden Mixture' in Noah's Day

In Rabbi Kirt Schneider's book *Decoding the Torah*, he touches on one particular command that seems quite strange. He calls it the Prohibition Against Forbidden Mixtures, a law in which the Lord said:

> **You shall keep my statutes. You shall not let your cattle breed with a different kind. You shall not sow your field with two kinds of seed, nor shall you wear a garment of cloth made of two kinds of material.**
>
> **— Leviticus 19:19 (*ESV*)**

When we think about "forbidden mixtures," one thing that quickly comes to mind is what happened at the time before the Flood. Genesis 6:1-4 tells us that in Noah's day, there was a population explosion, and the "sons of God," which we know from the book of Job and the Greek Septuagint are *fallen angels*, descended into the atmosphere of the earth, and they intermingled with women. From their forbidden sexual union, the women became pregnant and gave birth to a race of giants. The Bible calls them

Nephilim, and they were a mixed breed of terrestrial and celestial seed. To read more about this, Rick further covers this in detail in his book *Fallen Angels, Giants, Monsters, and the World Before the Flood.*

Genesis 6:4 says that there were giants in the earth in the days of Noah. Verse 5 explains "….that the wickedness of man was great in the earth, and that every imagination of the thoughts of his heart was only evil continually." The reason for this was the evil influence of the fallen angels and the forbidden mixture of their seed with humanity. God sent the Flood to purge the earth of all the corruption and violence brought about by these wicked entities and their offspring of giants. What took place in Noah's day is a prime example of what contradicted God's command in Leviticus 19:19.

Crossbreeding Animals and Plants Is Common Today

In a general sense, God's instructions in Leviticus 19:19 is forbidding mankind to tamper with His creation. He is calling us to respect the boundaries He has set forth as the Architect of the created world.

First, notice that God forbids the crossbreeding of animals. An example of animal crossbreeding today would be the mixing of seed between a wolf and a dog to create a *wolfdog*. Another example would be a *zonkey*, which is the result of mixing a male zebra and a female donkey, or a *liger*, which is the hybrid offspring of a male lion and a female tiger.

God didn't create any of these animals. Thus, they are a violation of the distinct species He built into his created world. Mankind may think it has come up with something ingenious, but in God's mind, it is a perversion that is dangerous.

Of course, many are familiar with the mixing of two plants together, such as the tomtato, which is the mixing of a tomato and a potato, or the cucamelon, which results from the crossing cucumber with watermelon. Although such experimentation may seem harmless, it has consequences. It's not just science or the evolution of plants. Essentially, God said, "No, I don't want you to mix species together."

What Is the Harm in Mixing Two Garments?

Why would the Lord tell us not to wear a garment made of both wool and linen together? In this case, there are three perspectives in Judaism we can draw from that are offered by ancient Jewish historians.

Perspective 1: We don't know exactly why God gave us this law of not wearing a garment made of wool and linen together, but the highest form of love and devotion is to obey Him even when we don't understand the reason.

Perspective 2: A second stream of Judaism says that historically, some idolatrous nations wore garments made of the mixing of wool and linen together, so the Lord didn't want His people to dress or look like the idolatrous nations.

Perspective 3: A third possibility is that this law has to do with not tampering with God's creation but respecting the distinctives. It's interesting to note that wool comes from a living animal, but linen comes from a plant. Remember, God wants His creation to reflect the order and distinction in which He created it.

Essentially, the Lord is calling us not to go beyond the boundaries He has built into the universe. Only He is all-knowing — we are not. For this reason alone, we need to know and respect His commands.

High-Tech Continues To Push the Boundaries

One of the greatest concerns today is the creation and rapid advancement of artificial intelligence, better known as AI. For several years, mankind has been working to create this new form of intellect through technology, but we have no idea what this new creation will do as it grows in strength and knowledge. No one knows for sure what is going to befall the world through its dominating presence.

When secular tech leaders like Elon Musk say that the creation of AI is like "summoning the demon," something is dreadfully wrong. The ramifications of what is coming in just the next five years are likely more grievous than anyone can think.

Transhumanism is also pushing the boundaries. In one sense, it seems like a good idea. When a person connects with a machine, and it helps restore their sight or their ability to use a limb they haven't been able to use, it is a good thing. But that's not the endgame of transhumanists. They want to take humanity to the next level and create a brand-new species that is part computer and part human. Ultimately, singularity is their goal — the intermingling of machinery and humanity into one. Through chip implants and certain Wi-Fi frequencies, the goal is for man to be one with "the cloud," having access to all the knowledge in the world. Is it a dream come true or humanity's worst nightmare?

Originally, God created everything to produce "after its own kind." That is what is repeatedly said in the creation account of Genesis 1. That's what is supposed to happen — that's God's will. However, His laws can be violated, which is exactly what we are seeing today. All kinds of laws are being violated, many of which we know nothing about.

Take, for example, what is happening in laboratories around the world. Scientists are mixing human DNA with that of animals. Specifically, we know for a fact that human DNA is being mixed with pig DNA. Initially, these efforts were for the purpose of growing human organs like kidneys and hearts inside of pigs that were to be given to patients on transplant lists.[1] But the experimentation hasn't stopped there. Researchers continue to push the boundaries looking to "see what they can do."

They're violating the laws of nature just like what happened in the days before the Flood when the fallen angels mixed with human women and it unleashed a race of horrific hybrid beings that brought unprecedented violence and bloodshed on the earth. God sent the Flood to cleanse the earth of this contamination. Ultimately, God will cleanse the earth again, this time using fire as the cleansing agent (*see* 2 Peter 3:7,10).

The End of Days
Are Like the Beginning of Days

Daniel 12 gives some vivid insights into what things are going to look like at the end of the age. In addition to talking about the Rapture, the Tribulation, and what's going to happen on the earth, he says that at the time of the end, "...Many shall run to and fro, and knowledge shall be increased" (Daniel 12:4).

This increase of knowledge describes the information age in which we now live, where human knowledge is said to now be doubling every 12 hours.[2] This exponential expansion of information includes things like transhumanism, hybridization, designer babies, and artificial intelligence (AI). All these things are wrapped up in knowledge. If you think about it, all of this goes back to the very beginning — to the tree of the knowledge of good and evil that was placed in the Garden of Eden.

Remember the story? God told man, "…Of every tree of the garden thou mayest freely eat: But of the tree of the knowledge of good and evil, thou shalt not eat of it: for in the day that thou eatest thereof thou shalt surely die" (Genesis 2:16-17).

Satan came along, cast doubt on God's command, and tempted Eve, by saying, "…You will not surely die. For God knows that in the day you eat of it your eyes will be opened, and you will be like God, knowing good and evil" (Genesis 3:4-5 *NKJV*). Eve swallowed the serpent's lie that somehow, by pushing past the boundary of God's command, everything in her life would be better and that she and Adam would be like God.

It's the same lie techno giants and transhumanists are peddling today. They say everything in our lives will be better, especially with the continued advancement of AI. Indeed, it appears to be improving healthcare, providing the development of new medicines and treatments, and solving problems we thought were unsolvable. Some even say that we will escape the clutches of death and become immortal — without any intervention from God.

With boasts like these, it's easy to see that nothing will stop AI's development. Indeed, it seems that artificial intelligence is Satan's bait to keep people from being authentically human anymore.

All this is a violation of God's command in Leviticus 19:19. It's tampering with God's creation in ways He told us not to. We are living in a time of thick, gross darkness, and it seems to be growing darker each day. That's why it is so important for us to walk with God and to know His laws. His abiding Spirit will empower us to resist the temptation and deception of the world.

We Live in a 'Trans' World

If you think about it, the world before the Flood was a world in *transgression*. Angelic beings and human beings were transgressing spiritual boundaries and transgressing biological boundaries at every turn. The giants, or Nephilim, were even said to be transgressing biological boundaries with animals, producing monstrous creatures. It was transgression after transgression after transgression.

Today, it is much the same. Transgression abounds. In fact, one of the biggest buzz words right now is **trans**. This includes the transgender movement and the transhumanism movement. Everywhere we look, there is a deliberate violation of God's laws and standards. But these violations are being presented by Satan in a similar way the serpent deceived Eve into taking the forbidden fruit. "Let's shake off the shackles of the past," the enemy says. "This is 'a new day of enlightenment.'" But the truth is, we are simply transgressing God's laws and mixing things we shouldn't.

What is interesting is that some ancient rabbis taught that mixing wool and linen together — that is, the crossbreeding and blurring of God's ordained lines of distinctions — is similar to releasing the forces of Cain and Abel. In other words, it's a very dangerous thing. When we mix what God designed to be separate, it is as if we unleash murderous demonic spirits. Although we're not suggesting that this is in any way a scientific reality, what we are stating is that we need to understand what's happening right now and be mindful about how the world is using technology.

What Can We Do in These Volatile Times?

The severity of the times in which we live begs the question, "What can we do to escape all this?" Things seem to just keep getting more and more intense, and our lives keep getting busier and more complicated with each passing day. Many people — including some believers — are getting sucked deeper into relying on technology. Again, this makes us ask, "Where can we go to escape all this? Is there a place where we can move off the grid and live in nature, disconnected from the internet and our cell phones? Can we possibly go back to an agrarian lifestyle and just live in God's natural world?"

Although there are some choices we can and should make to disentangle from the things of this world and live a simpler life, there seems to be no way to fully escape the age of escalating change in which we live. The only time-tested answers for dealing with the myriad of issues we're facing are:

- **Feed on God's Word.**
- **Stay filled with the Holy Spirit.**
- **Grow strong in the Lord and in the power of His might now!**

- **Cultivate healthy relationships.**

As you listen to the voice of the Holy Spirit, He will lead and guide you as to what boundaries you need to establish in your life. For example, what are God's limits for you in using AI and researching things on the Internet? What movies, music, and TV shows are good for you and your family to watch and listen to and which ones should you delete from your media menu? The Holy Spirit will instruct you and teach you regarding these things and help you not transgress a boundary that would be spiritually unhealthy or a detriment to you and others. The last thing any of us want to do is fall under the spell of great deception that's proliferating in the world today.

Keep Close Company With Godly People

We also need to make sure that we are in the company of God-focused, sound-minded people, which means we need to periodically take an inventory of who we're hanging out with and who is influencing us. This precaution is summed up in God's law found in Exodus 23:32-33 (*NASB1995*), where God said:

> **You shall make no covenant with them or with their gods. They shall not live in your land, because they will make you sin against Me; for if you serve their gods, it will surely be a snare to you.**

Sadly, many good-meaning people — including many Christians — are ensnared by their friends. They are keeping close company with the wrong people who are making wrong choices, and if they don't sever these types of relationships, it will end up costing them dearly. That is why God warned the children of Israel immediately after He delivered them from slavery not to make a covenant with any heathen people or their gods.

The word "covenant" in Exodus 23:32 describes *a political alliance or economic alliance*. That is what God commanded Israel not to form with ungodly nations, but they did it anyway. As a result, they became weak, and God judged them for their disobedience. Israel's example demonstrates the danger of moral relativism. If we accept the ungodly values of the people around us and adopt them as our own, we will be made weak and reap the consequences of a curse because we've disobeyed the Lord. Even worse, we will end up losing our distinct calling as God's priests in the earth.

Focus on God and Cling to Him Alone

In Hebrew, the word for "focus" is *kavanaugh*. If we don't learn to keep our focus on God alone for everything we need, we will default to relying on the world or another entity to meet our needs and keep us strong. And if we're not relying on God alone, we're going to experience the same negative effects that happened to Israel when they made alliances with heathen nations and heathen gods. Just as they were scattered and lost their place, we will be scattered and lose our place.

Rather than look to others as our source, God wants us to look to Him and *cling* to Him! In Hebrew, the word for "clinging" is *devekut*. Although the temptation to rely on the world to affirm us, accept us, and meet our needs is certainly strong and something people often do, God wants us to draw our affirmation, our acceptance, and our strength directly from Him.

Unfortunately, rather than standing out in the world and clinging to God alone for affirmation and acceptance, what many people do is begin to subtly adjust what they know in their heart is right, allowing morality and truth to become relative and adaptable. They begin to compromise their heartfelt, God-given convictions in the way they walk and talk, in the choices they make, and in what they allow into their home.

Keep in mind, in Exodus 23:33, God said that ungodly people, "...shall not live in your land, because they will make you sin against Me...." For us, our "land" includes the home in which we live and our very person.

If you're allowing the world's pollution to stream into your home through movies, music, television, the Internet, and your relationships, it is the equivalent of making an alliance with ungodly people and allowing them to "live in your land." If at first it pained you to see and hear certain things, but over time through repeated exposure, you've become desensitized and calloused to it, you have lost your spiritual sensitivity.

If you can freely watch and hear things that once grieved you, you're going in the wrong direction. Compromising and lowering your standards to have "friends" and be "entertained" grieves the heart of God and will eventually make you sin against Him. It's time to heed God's warning in Exodus 23:32-33 and stay separate from the world.

Establish and Maintain Biblical Boundaries

There is a price for this separation. Jesus said:

> **If you were of the world, the world would love its own; but because you are not of the world, but I chose you out of the world, because of this the world hates you.**
> — **John 15:19** (*NASB1995*)

Friend, God wants us to stand strong, be separate, and "abstain from pollutions of idols" (Acts 15:20). An idol is anything that we have in our life that is a substitute for God or tries to take His place in our life. When we flirt with the things of this world, we are flirting with things polluted by idols, and it brings spiritual filth or contamination into our life.

Through Peter, God told the Early Church to be holy and separate unto Him. He said, "…Be ye holy; for I am holy" (1 Peter 1:16). This calling hasn't changed. God has called all of us out of darkness into His marvelous light (*see* 1 Peter 2:9). We are not supposed to flirt with darkness. Instead, we are to draw a line in the sand and establish immovable boundaries between us and everything that is not of God. Yes, we need to have mercy and compassion for those around us, but we also need to determine what we're going to do and not do, what we're going to permit and not permit, because we are God's holy people.

A practical example of how this principle might apply is in the selection of where we send our children to school and college. This can be a difficult decision for parents. The reality is most public schools and colleges today are not teaching or promoting the ways of God. In many respects, sending our children and young people to public schools and universities is like sending them to be educated in a heathen nation. By and large, the value system being taught is contrary to — and in some cases, downright hostile to — walking in alignment with God's Word. If you're at this crossroads with your kids, pray and seek the Lord for His divine wisdom. He will show you the best way to choose (*see* Psalm 25:12).

Entering the right business relationship can also be a challenging thing. To be in partnership with others means to come into agreement with them. The same is true about investing financially in a company. When it comes to making money, sometimes people discard their morals and ethics and bow their knee to the god of money. Before we form an alliance and go into business with someone and before we make an investment into someone's company, we need to be aware of who that person is, what he believes in, and what he stands for.

The bottom line is that God is calling us to live a life that's holy and separate to Him. If we will live our life surrendered to Him and acknowledge Him in all our ways, He will direct our path and bless our lives in indescribable ways!

STUDY QUESTIONS

Study to shew thyself approved unto God, a workman that needeth not to be ashamed, rightly dividing the word of truth.
— 2 Timothy 2:15

1. Eve bought the serpent's lie and believed that by pushing past the boundary of God's command, everything in her life would be better. How about you? Is there something the enemy is dangling in front of you that you know God said to stay away from? Are you tempted to push past God's boundary and do it anyway? Carefully read Genesis 3 and listen for what the Holy Spirit speaks to you from this timeless example.

2. Friend, God wants us to stand strong, be separate, and "abstain from pollutions of idols" (*see* Acts 15:20). Are there any "idols" in your life? While you're likely not bowing to golden images or carved statues, sometimes there are things that we unknowingly elevate to a higher level of importance than God. Consider the explanation of idols in First John 5:21 (*AMPC*):

    Little children, keep yourselves from idols (false gods) — [from anything and everything that would occupy the place in your heart due to God, from any sort of substitute for Him that would take first place in your life]. Amen (so let it be).

    What is the Holy Spirit showing you about your life from this verse? Is there anything that has taken His place? If so, repent (*see* 1 John 1:9) and ask Him for His grace to keep Him in first place in your life.

3. Although we can't fully escape the tumultuous age in which we live, there are proven actions God tells us to take in His Word to live victoriously and stay spiritually strong. Consider these words of priceless wisdom:

- **Feed on God's Word** (John 8:31-32; Deuteronomy 8:3; Jeremiah 15:16; 1 Peter 2:2; Acts 20:32; Hebrews 4:12; Colossians 3:16; James 1:21-25).

- **Stay filled with the Holy Spirit** (Acts 1:8; Ephesians 5:18; 6:18; Jude 20; Micah 3:8; Zechariah 4:6).

- **Grow strong in the Lord and in the power of His might** (Ephesians 6:10-18).

- **Cultivate healthy relationships** (Ecclesiastes 4:9-12; Proverbs 13:20; 17:17; 27:17).

PRACTICAL APPLICATION

But be ye doers of the word, and not hearers only, deceiving your own selves.
— James 1:22

1. In this world of deep darkness and deception, the Holy Spirit is here to lead and guide you as to what boundaries you need to establish. Pause and pray, "Lord, help me. Show me and my family what movies, music, TV shows, and Internet sites are good for us to watch and listen to and which ones we need to avoid. Help us hear and obey Your voice regarding the use of AI. Please instruct us and teach us regarding all things and help us not transgress a boundary that would be a detriment to us. In Jesus' name, amen!"

2. It's been said, "Show me your friends, and I will show you your future." Just as hanging out in a smoke-filled room will make you smell like smoke, the people you spend a lot of time with are going to affect your life. Stop and think, *Who are my close friends? Is there anyone I'm hanging out with that is causing me to compromise the standards of God's Word and leading me away from Him?* As you ponder these questions, consider the following scriptures and ask the Holy Spirit to help you clearly see what changes you need to make in the company you keep. (*See* 1 Corinthians 15:33, 5:11; Numbers 33:51-52,55; Proverbs 4:14; 22:24-25; Psalm 1:1; 2 Corinthians 6:14-18.)

---

[1]A Pioneer: Human-Pig Chimera Successfully Grows Humanized Kidneys (https://www.cornellhealthcarereview.org/post/a-pioneer-human-pig-chimera-successfully-grows-humanized-kidneys; accessed 7/24/25).

[2]Knowledge Velocity (https://jimcarroll.substack.com/p/knowledge-velocity; accessed 7/24/25).

LESSON 5

TOPIC

Are You Following the Crowd?

SCRIPTURES

1. **Exodus 23:2** (*NASB1995*) — You shall not follow the masses in doing evil, nor shall you testify in a dispute so as to turn aside after a multitude in order to pervert justice.

2. **Leviticus 22:31-33** (*NASB1995*) — So you shall keep My commandments, and do them; I am the Lord. "You shall not profane My holy name, but I will be sanctified among the sons of Israel; I am the Lord who sanctifies you, who brought you out from the land of Egypt, to be your God; I am the Lord."

3. **Leviticus 19:17** (*NASB1995*) — You shall not hate your fellow countryman in your heart; you may surely reprove your neighbor, but shall not incur sin because of him.

4. **Deuteronomy 16:14** (*NASB1995*) — And you shall rejoice in your feast, you and your son and your daughter and your male and female servants and the Levite and the stranger and the orphan and the widow who are in your towns.

GREEK/HEBREW WORDS

No Greek or Hebrew words were shown on the TV program.

SYNOPSIS

One of the beautiful things about Judaism is that a great deal of time has been spent on analyzing every single word of the Scriptures. As a result, we are able to extract a tremendous amount of truth that goes far beyond just the surface meaning. That is what we will see as we go through this final lesson on *Decoding the Torah*. We will unpack what it means to profane God's name, how and when we're to bring correction to others, and the value of heeding God's command to rejoice and be happy.

The emphasis of this lesson:

By following Jesus, we're going to be in opposition to society. While the world sees nothing wrong with profaning God's name, He commands us not to do anything that would cause Him to be disrespected. He also instructs us to reprove those with whom we're in relation and to develop a happy disposition, which brings completeness, wholeness, and perfection.

As Christians, We're To Live in Sync With Christ Not the Crowd

As we continue in our study of *Decoding the Torah*, we want to look at another command God gave to His people through Moses, and it is found in Exodus 23:2 (*NASB1995*). Here God said:

> **You shall not follow the masses in doing evil, nor shall you testify in a dispute so as to turn aside after a multitude in order to pervert justice.**

If there was ever a law that applied to today, it is this one. No doubt, we're living in a culture of compromise — a world that is drifting further and further from God's moral truth. Nevertheless, to see God giving a command to His people in the ancient Torah to not follow an evil majority, brings strength to us to stand strong in our own day.

Of course, going against the grain of the masses is not popular and will quickly cause us to be alienated from the world around us. But we need to stand strong and maintain our identity in Christ, which means being separate from the world. That is who we are called to be — people who are consecrated and set apart to God. That is the Bible's definition of what it means to be a "saint."

Although you may not have heard much teaching on it, the Bible says that part of our calling is to be rejected with Jesus. But if we suffer rejection with Him, we will also reign with Him (*see* 2 Timothy 2:12). So don't allow yourself to compromise and adopt the value system of the culture. Instead, by the grace of God, endure criticism and make decisions that honor God and uphold His Word, even if it separates you and makes you feel like the odd man out.

Rabbi Schneider shared how during COVID, he made a personal decision not to receive the vaccine, and the reason was threefold. First, he had already contracted COVID, so he trusted in his own body's ability to build immunity. Second, he personally didn't trust the vaccine because it was brand new and barely tested. Third, he felt like doing so would hinder his relationship with God.

Even though Rabbi Schneider had good friends that chose to get the vaccine, for him to take it would have been a violation of his own heart and bowing down to the culture's demands. Sadly, because of his decision, he received pressure from his doctor, several healthcare professionals, as well as from his family and friends. Yet, although he was criticized and ostracized for his decision, he would not give in to the intimidating weight of the prevailing culture.

If you are following Jesus, you need to get used to being unpopular and in a class all alone with Him. Indeed, as Christians, we are a "peculiar people" (1 Peter 2:9), and there's nothing wrong with that.

What Does It Mean To 'Profane God's Name'?

In the Ten Commandments that the Lord gave Moses to give to His people, the third commandment says, "Thou shalt not take the name of the Lord thy God in vain..." (Exodus 20:7). It is interesting to note that this command seems to be echoed and expanded in the book of Leviticus, where God said:

> **So you shall keep My commandments, and do them; I am the Lord. You shall not profane My holy name, but I will be sanctified among the sons of Israel; I am the Lord who sanctifies you, who brought you out from the land of Egypt, to be your God; I am the Lord.**
> **— Leviticus 22:31-33 (*NASB1995*)**

After God said to keep His commandments, He said, "...You shall not profane My holy name..." (Leviticus 22:32). When most people think about "profaning" God's name, they think of using it as a curse word, and that is certainly an example of profaning. But degrading God's name is much broader than just using His name as a swear word. In fact, there are several ways we as God's people can profane His name without recognizing it.

First, we profane God's name when we refer to Him or speak about Him casually. For example, simply saying, "Oh God!" as an idiom of common speech when something happens is profaning His name. Although many believers use this expression and don't mean any disrespect, it is, nevertheless, profaning God's name because it is using it casually in a social context rather than revering it and honoring it as holy.

A second way that we can profane God's name is by professing to be believers but then living in an ungodly way. For instance, if we declare that we're believers, but our conversation is filled with a lot of complaining and murmuring, or criticizing and judging others, we are profaning God's name. The same is true when we adopt an attitude of arrogance and entitlement. These attitudes and actions degrade and dishonor the name of God and Jesus His Son.

A third way we can profane God's name and use it in vain is by attributing things to Him that He did not do. One rabbi said an example of this is saying that earthquakes, tornadoes, hurricanes, and the like are "acts of God." Although that's what insurance companies call them, none of these things are acts of God — they're acts of nature. Because of man's sin, death and destruction entered the world, and creation was subjected to brokenness and corruption (*see* Romans 8:20-22). When we attribute disastrous things to God, we are, in a way, using His name in vain.

Another, more straightforward, way of profaning God's name is when a person says to someone, "I swear to God." How many times have we heard someone say, "If I tell you something, you have to swear to God you won't tell anyone"? That's profaning God's name. Jesus said, clearly, "…Do not swear at all: neither by heaven, for it is God's throne; nor by the earth, for it is His footstool; nor by Jerusalem, for it is the city of the great King…. But let your 'Yes' be 'Yes,' and your 'No,' 'No.' For whatever is more than these is from the evil one" (Matthew 5:34-35,37 *NKJV*).

Basically, anything we do that causes God to be disrespected is profaning His name.

In Hebrew, the phrase "birkat Hashem" means *to curse, profane, or disrespect the Lord's name*. The opposite of this is "kadosh Hashem," which means *to sanctify God's name*. The way that we sanctify God's name is to treat it as holy and do our best to live in such a way that we're glorifying Him in our lives. This is the second part of the law in Leviticus 22:32 and what truly blesses the heart of God.

'Reproving Your Neighbor'
Is a Command of God

There is another law we don't hear much about, but it is extremely important. It has to do with bringing correction to those with whom you are in relationship, and it is found in Leviticus 19:17 (*NASB1995*), where the Lord says:

> **You shall not hate your fellow countryman in your heart; you may surely reprove your neighbor, but shall not incur sin because of him.**

The most important thing to know about this command is that it is given to us by God in the context of love for the purpose of restoring broken relationships. The fact that God tells us not to hate our "fellow countryman" in our heart *before* He tells us to reprove him shows His desire to preserve the bond of love we have for one another.

Unfortunately, what many people do when their "neighbor" does something that hurts or offends them is they build a wall between them and that person *or* they go to them in anger and verbally attack them for what they did.

The fact of the matter is that the "neighbor" may not even realize what they did was hurtful. Likewise, the person who was hurt or offended may have misunderstood the whole situation. But rather than going to their neighbor and calmly telling them that what they did offended them, they hold onto the offense and become bitter, or they go to them and blow up in anger.

Again, God's heart is to preserve the bond of peace and love and restore our relationships.

That said, imagine a friend or family member really hurt you by something they did. The right way to handle it is to go to them and say, "When you said that to me the other day, it really hurt me," or "It really bothered me and made me uncomfortable." You are to bring the situation to them in a non-threatening, non-provoking way with the goal of clearing the air and making things right. The last thing you want to do is verbally attack them and tell them how "mad" they made you. All that is going to do is light a fire of anger and rage that incites your "neighbor" to aggressively retaliate.

Done correctly, what generally happens is that the person who hurt or offended you will begin to explain what they did and why they did it. Usually, it is a learning opportunity for you and them. You will probably see something you misunderstood, and they'll hopefully apologize for hurting you and try to change their behavior. In most cases, the issue will be resolved and the relationship restored.

So instead of just letting a hurtful situation fester in your heart, which builds walls and separates you from others, prayerfully deal with the grievance and pray for God to restore the broken relationship. Many disputes and frustrations in relationships can be resolved if you will just go to the person that hurt you and talk to them honestly and respectfully about it.

When and When *Not* To Rebuke

At this point you may be saying, "Who is my neighbor?" People asked Jesus this same question, and essentially, His answer was *everyone*.

Of course, there is a right time and a wrong time to go to someone and bring correction, and the key is knowing when the time is right and then addressing the issue in the right way.

If someone you're working with or in relationship with is doing something repeatedly that's upsetting you and it's likely to keep happening, you should go talk to that person about it. If what he (or she) did happened one time or was trivial and not likely to happen again, you probably shouldn't go to that person and correct him. Ask God for His grace to just let it go.

Remember, you've done things in the past that unknowingly hurt or offended others, and you'll most likely do something hurtful again. You too will need and want mercy for your wrong attitudes and actions, so plant some seeds of forgiveness now that you can reap a harvest of later.

Nevertheless, if what someone did is likely to continue to happen and disrupt your relationship — or harm other people — you need to pray for the right time and the right words to reprove that person. You must also bring correction when you notice someone is behaving in a way that's hurting other people or alienating them from others. If you see it's a problem that you could resolve constructively by confronting them or rebuking the person in love, you should go to him.

To be clear, you should never go rebuke or correct someone if you are not emotionally ready. In other words, if you're angry and enraged at someone and you go to him and spew words of anger and hate, the result will be worse. That is not the right time to rebuke that person. You need to wait to get your head on straight.

Furthermore, you should not rebuke someone if it's unsafe. In other words, if the person in the wrong is volatile and not in his (or her) right mind to receive correction and confronting him is going to put you in a position where this person can physically harm you, it's probably wise not to confront that person but to figure out another way to deal with the situation.

Rejoicing and Being Happy Is a Command From God

As we wrap up our study, there is one more command God gave in the Torah we want to touch on, and it is the law to be happy. It is found in the book of Deuteronomy, and here the Lord says:

> **And you shall rejoice in your feast, you and your son and your daughter and your male and female servants and the Levite and the stranger and the orphan and the widow who are in your towns.**
> **— Deuteronomy 16:14 (*NASB1995*)**

Believe it or not, there is a great deal of instruction in both the Old Testament and New Testament about having joy and being happy. In this verse, the Lord is actually commanding His people to rejoice before Him and be happy, and they were to celebrate all the good things He had done and was doing for them. Similarly, as New Testament believers, He calls us to rejoice and celebrate His goodness too.

The enemy is always wanting us to look at things negatively. He wants us to see the glass as half empty rather than half full. The fact is, if we're focused on this world, we're going to see its many problems, which is extremely discouraging and exactly what Satan wants. Knowing that God desires us to be happy and commands us to rejoice gives us ample reason to shift our will into agreement with His.

By nature, God is happy and filled with joy. That is why Paul said, "I pray that God, the source of hope, will fill you completely with **joy** and **peace** because you trust in him. Then you will overflow with confident hope through the power of the Holy Spirit" (Romans 15:13 *NLT*).

As one man said, **A person is only as happy as they make up their mind to be.**

There is a great deal of truth in that statement. It seems to echo Proverbs 23:7, which says, "For as he thinketh in his heart, so is he...." By the power of the Holy Spirit, we need to find a way to focus on what is good, true, right, and worthy of praise and to choose to be as happy as possible.

God Wants Us To Practice Being Happy

There is something quite fascinating about when the Lord revealed His name to Moses in the book of Exodus. After God commanded Moses to go to Israel and speak to them on His behalf, the Bible says:

> **Then Moses said to God, "Indeed, when I come to the children of Israel and say to them, 'The God of your fathers has sent me to you,' and they say to me, 'What is His name?' what shall I say to them?"**

> **And God said to Moses, "I AM WHO I AM." And He said, "Thus you shall say to the children of Israel, 'I AM has sent me to you.'"**
>
> **— Exodus 3:13-14 (*NKJV*)**

Then in His next breath, God said to Moses:

> **"...Say this to the people of Israel: *Yahweh*, the God of your ancestors — the God of Abraham, the God of Isaac, and the God of Jacob — has sent me to you. This is my eternal name, my name to remember for all generations."**
>
> **— Exodus 3:15 (*NLT*)**

So the name *Yahweh* — which is the Hebrew word for "I AM WHO I AM" — became God's sacred, covenant name forever. If you think about the name "I AM WHO I AM," it indicates that God is beyond time. He fills up the *past*, He fills up the *present*, and He fills up the *future*. "I AM WHO I AM" fills all dimensions of time.

Time is divided into *three* parts — past, present, and future — and the number three is very significant. The patriarchs of our faith referred to by God are *three* in number — Abraham, Isaac, and Jacob. When you think about the tabernacle where the Lord met His people, it is made of *three* sections: the outer court, the Holy Place, and the Holy of Holies. Likewise, when you think about how the Lord revealed Himself to us in the New Testament, He did it as Father, Son, and Holy Spirit. Again, we have *three*.

What is the significance of three? Because God's commandment to rejoice and be happy were tied to three pilgrim festivals or feasts of Israel: Passover, Pentecost, and Tabernacles. These festivals were also known as the *Feast of Unleavened Bread*, the *Feast of Weeks*, and the *Feast of Tabernacles*.

Again, the Lord said, "And You shall rejoice in your feast, you and your son and your daughter, your male servant and your female servant and the Levite, the stranger and the fatherless and the widow, who are within your gates.... *Three* times a year all your males shall appear before the Lord your God in the place which He chooses: at the Feast of Unleavened Bread, at the Feast of Weeks, and at the Feast of Tabernacles..." (Deuteronomy 16:14-16 *NKJV*).

The number three represents *completeness*, *wholeness*, and *perfection*.

What all of this is telling us is that if God commanded His people to rejoice, be happy, and celebrate three times a year — and three represents completeness, wholeness, and perfection — we should work with the Holy Spirit to develop a disposition to regularly rejoice, be happy, and celebrate all the time. Indeed, as God's people, we should practice being happy. It is a daily, sometimes moment-by-moment decision, and it is rooted in being thankful.

So when you're feeling down and discouraged, count your blessings — name them one by one. God will hear you, and His heart will be so touched, He Himself will fill you with His joy and peace through your faith and trust in Him!

STUDY QUESTIONS

Study to shew thyself approved unto God, a workman that needeth not to be ashamed, rightly dividing the word of truth. — 2 Timothy 2:15

1. According to Matthew 22:36-40 and Mark 12:28-31, what did Jesus say is the first and greatest commandment and the second, which is

much like it? (Note: These are taken directly from Deuteronomy 6:4-5 and Leviticus 19:18 in the Torah.)

2. God's command to "reprove your neighbor" in Leviticus 19:17 (*NASB1995*) is a lot like what Jesus said in the gospels. Take a few moments to carefully reflect on His words in Matthew 5:23-24; 18:15-17; and Luke 17:3-4, and in your own words, describe what Jesus said is the right way to deal with people who hurt you. (As you answer, consider Mark 11:25; Ephesians 4:32; Colossians 3:13.)

3. What we focus on is of paramount importance, especially when it comes to cultivating a happy heart. Proverbs 23:7 says, "For as he thinketh in his heart, *so is he....*" What does God instruct us to fix our mind on in Isaiah 26:3-4; Joshua 1:8; Hebrews 12:2-3; and Philippians 4:8? And what blessings can you expect from this practice?

PRACTICAL APPLICATION

**But be ye doers of the word, and not hearers only,
deceiving your own selves.**
— James 1:22

1. Reread the section on what it means to *profane God's name* and then ask the Lord to examine your heart. Are there any areas in your life that the Holy Spirit is revealing where you've been unknowingly dishonoring or desecrating God's name? If so, receive His conviction and ask Him to forgive you. Then ask Him to show you practical ways to treat His name as holy and live in such a way that you're glorifying Him in and through your life.

2. If someone has hurt you deeply and/or repeatedly, you're probably still dealing with the emotional pain and anger over what he or she did. You may even be unknowingly holding onto offense and unforgiveness. To move forward and experience all the good things God has in store for you, make the choice to begin the process of forgiveness.

Biblical Steps to Walking in Forgiveness

- Admit that you're offended and with whom.
  (Proverbs 28:13; Ezekiel 18:31; 1 John 1:7-10)

- Release the person and their offense to God; make the daily choice to forgive.
  (Matthew 6:14-15; Mark 11:25; Ephesians 4:32; Colossians 3:13)

- Ask for and receive God's forgiveness for holding on to offense and unforgiveness.
  (1 John 1:9; Psalm 32:1-6; Proverbs 28:13; Acts 3:19)

- Bless the person who hurt you; as an act of your will, pray for God to bless him or her.
  (Matthew 5:44-45; Romans 12:14; 1 Peter 3:8-12)

Remember, forgiving someone is a *process*, so repeat these steps as often as necessary, especially when thoughts of what he or she did return and/ or you feel negative emotions trying to rise up and take root again. God will honor and bless your efforts to walk in forgiveness!

A Prayer To Receive Salvation

If you've never received Jesus as your Savior and Lord, now is the time for you to experience the new life Jesus wants to give you! To receive God's gift of salvation that can be obtained through Jesus alone, pray this prayer from your heart:

Jesus, I repent of my sin and receive You as my Savior and Lord. Wash away my sin with Your precious blood and make me completely new. I thank You that my sin is removed, and Satan no longer has any right to lay claim on me. Through Your empowering grace, I faithfully promise that I will serve You as my Lord for the rest of my life.

If you just prayed this prayer of salvation, you are born again! You are a brand-new creation in Christ! Would you please let us know of your decision by going to **renner.org/salvation**? We would love to connect with you and pray for you as you begin your new life in Christ.

Scriptures for further study: John 3:16; John 14:6; Acts 4:12; Ephesians 1:7; Hebrews 10:19,20; 1 Peter 1:18,19; Romans 10:9,10; Colossians 1:13; 2 Corinthians 5:17; Romans 6:4; 1 Peter 1:3

Notes

CLAIM YOUR FREE RESOURCE!

As a way of introducing you further to the teaching ministry of Rick Renner, we would like to send you FREE of charge his teaching, "How To Receive a Miraculous Touch From God" on CD or as an MP3 download.

In His earthly ministry, Jesus commonly healed *all* who were sick of *all* their diseases. In this profound message, learn about the manifold dimensions of Christ's wisdom, goodness, power, and love toward all humanity who came to Him in faith with their needs.

☑ YES, I want to receive Rick Renner's monthly teaching letter!

Simply scan the QR code to claim this resource or go to: **renner.org/claim-your-free-offer**

Connect

WITH US!

www.ingramcontent.com/pod-product-compliance
Lightning Source LLC
Chambersburg PA
CBHW071642040426
42452CB00009B/1729